UNDERSTAND
HOW TO DRAW DS10

# Exploring
# Effects in Drawing

## Peter Caldwell

**SEARCH PRESS**

# Introduction

Although drawing and painting are the most enjoyable and rewarding experiences, the road to improvement is a gradual one. In fact, the overcoming of problems can give rise to a greater sense of achievement than the final picture. The story of Michelangelo Buonarroti's life, *The Agony and the Ecstasy*, is aptly entitled.

Most artists, whether amateur or professional, have their own problem areas. Amateurs give as much time as they can spare to practising, reading books, and attending art courses to find the magic formula for success. It has to be said at the outset that no magic wand exists to wave over an unsatisfactory picture and the idea that there must somehow be a way to overcome a lack of talent is an illusion. Professional artists spend most of their lives involved with the task of achieving the best possible effect, using all their skill and know-how which has accumulated over many years of dedicated work. Most of them would admit, however, that they have their own trade secrets or, put another way, short cuts to achieving effects.

Exploring effects in drawing is the subject of this book and whilst I hope that you will be eager to try some of the techniques in your own work, do not be deceived into thinking that these effects are easy. You will still need to practise and adapt the methods to your own pictures, no doubt improving upon my suggestions and devising even better ways of your own. Of course, staleness will be inevitable if you only tackle easy subjects in a medium that is too familiar. Do not become complacent but try difficult themes from time to time, using different media. Within the limitations of this small book, I illustrate some of the effects that are possible using drawing tools alone.

*A bunch of grapes created simply by dipping the flat, unsharpened end of a pencil into some diluted ink and then pressing it on to the paper.*

# Materials and their effects

Although most of my work is done in the studio, I enjoy sketching outdoors as much as possible. The reason for this, apart from travelling around and seeing new subjects, is the spontaneity and freshness of the drawing. Working at home can encourage a leisured approach, resulting in tightness and overprecision.

The variety of papers and drawing implements available to the artist, whether working indoors or outside, seems limitless and this makes any choice of materials difficult. I suggest, therefore, that you try out as many different materials as possible, both to explore the range of effects that can be achieved from the various media and also to discover the ones with which you feel happiest. To help you, a list of the basic items and their qualities is given here.

*A loose pencil sketch on cartridge paper, using a grade 4B pencil.*

*A quick, on-the-spot pencil sketch for future reference.*

### Drawing implements

Remember, a drawing tool is only an extension of your hand and should feel comfortable.

**Pencils** No list would be complete without the pencil, the most versatile and satisfying of all media. It will do everything from a small rough sketch or doodle to much larger finished drawings. Pencils are graded according to hardness and softness; H to 6H being the hardest, HB medium, then B to 6B the softest. I prefer to use the HB and B grades and, in fact, over the years I have found myself using mostly 2B and 4B. The side of the lead is as pleasant to draw with as the point; use the side for shading, and the point for outline and detail. I always keep a few sharpened pencils next to my drawing, one for detail and the others for shading. If you use only one pencil, then you will be forever sharpening the point!

**Carbon pencils** These are excellent for large, bold, free drawings, or for very soft rich textures, but they are not easy to sharpen for detailed work. Care must be taken not to smudge your work, and a fixative must be used on the finished work.

**Charcoal pencils** These are more or less the same as carbon pencils but are more easily sharpened for detail. I use the two pencils together – the carbon pencil for large broad surfaces and the charcoal pencil to add any necessary details.

*A carbon pencil sketch on cartridge paper gives a loose, free expression to the subject. The rough, irregular line imparts a great sense of liveliness.*

*Old engine in black water-soluble pencil on cartridge paper. Some lines and areas have been softened with a sable brush and clean water.*

**Water-soluble pencils** Do not overlook the water-soluble pencil, which happens to be another of my favourite tools. This is a very versatile medium, as it allows you not only to do a straightforward drawing, but also to add a variety of tonal effects simply by brushing clean water into certain areas.

**Conté crayons and pencils** These give a very rich, soft texture. The crayons are available in square sticks about 7cm (2½in) long and come in three grades; soft, medium, and hard. Usually, I break off a piece of the stick about 2cm (¾in) long and, holding it between my thumb and forefinger, use it to give hard and soft sweeping strokes alternately, according to the amount of pressure that I apply. There seems to be no end to the variety of interesting effects that can be achieved with practice.

*To give emphasis to the strokes, pressure can be applied either to the left or the right side of the conté crayon. Use bold, curved or downward strokes and never try to draw with an upward motion. If you have to draw upwards, then it is better to turn the drawing upside-down.*

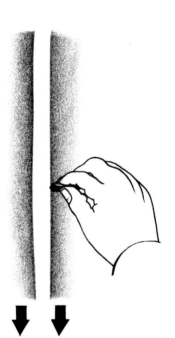

*Holding the conté pencil between the thumb and forefinger gives lovely rich, textured strokes. This medium is ideal for quick, simple drawings, but it must be sprayed with a fixative to prevent it from smudging.*

**Pens** When drawing with ink, you must decide exactly what you want to do and then do it positively, because pen strokes cannot be erased easily. There are many varieties of pens on the market these days, so once again it is very important to try out as many as possible.

**Dip-pens** These are what the name suggests; a flexible nib in a holder, which has to be constantly dipped into the ink. Even though this can seem to be a bit of a chore, the flexible nib allows the artist to draw with a sensitive variation of line according to the pressure applied.

**Cartridge pens** These are available in a wide variety of nib sizes and are convenient to use because they do not require constant filling.

*Some sketch-book studies of boats, using a graphic needle-point pen.*

*A dip-pen sketch on Bristol board.*

**Graphic needle-point pens** These give a fine, even line and are easy to use. They are made with either waterproof or water-soluble ink. I use the waterproof ink version quite frequently so that I can then use watercolour washes over the top.

**Fibre and felt-tipped pens** Both of these are very handy for on-the-spot sketches. Even when the pens are starting to lose their strength, they produce a nice soft greyish line which can still be used for shading. Finished sketches can be enhanced with crayons, pastels, or by brushing in some watercolour.

7

## Papers

There is a vast range of papers from which to choose, in qualities suitable for every medium, so experiment in order to find the surfaces with which you feel happiest. Drawing paper ranges through the whole spectrum, from ultra-smooth to very rough. The conventional qualities are listed here, together with a few not so obvious choices which are just as pleasant to draw on and, in some instances, lend a certain charm to the work.

**Cartridge paper** This is the most popular paper for drawing and sketching, and it is available in a variety of different surfaces; smooth, semi-smooth, and rough.

**Bristol board** This is a very smooth white board which comes in various thicknesses and is used for pen drawings.

**Ingres paper** This has a soft, furry surface which is ideal for pastel drawings and is made in an extremely wide range of colours, including grey, pink, cream, blue, buff, and green.

**Sketch-books** These are amongst the most indispensable items in every artist's equipment. All the papers listed so far can be obtained in sketch-book form.

**White wallpaper lining paper** This is great for big, loose charcoal pencil drawings. A whole roll of lining paper cut up into convenient sizes works out quite inexpensive as well!

**Typing paper** This provides a nice smooth surface for pencil sketching. Make up your own sketch-book with a ring-binder.

**Brown wrapping paper** Using the non-shiny side with the feint lines gives a lovely surface for pen, pencil, or pastel work. As the paper is a pleasant buff brown colour, highlights can be picked out with white pencil, crayon, or paint.

*In this drawing of an elephant I have used a combination of black, grey, and white pastels on a light grey Ingres paper.*

*Cumbrian village. Pen and ink on smooth, grey tinted board, with white gouache paint in selected areas to give added interest.*

*French pavement café in pen and ink.*

# Creating effects with basic techniques

I have done this drawing especially to show a representative sample of textures and the techniques used to create them. It is important to point out that what I have attempted to do in this drawing is by no means the be-all and end-all, but simply my way of creating texture in this particular subject. In another drawing I might choose to use different ways of achieving interesting effects.

*Although this is a very busy little drawing with a lot of detail, much of it is suggested. For example, there is just the suggestion of bricks. There is no need to put them all in, as the odd brick shaded in here and there is quite sufficient.*

*The dark tracery of branches within the foliage is interesting, and it is well worth the effort to accentuate them. Notice the slight swelling where one branch or twig joins another. They really look as if they grow out of each other and are not just stuck on.*

*Although there are millions of leaves on the tree, I have left the sunlit areas of the foliage as white paper and put the density of detail into the dark shadows only.*

*Windows always offer a challenge to make them look lively and highly reflective. Concentrate the swirling black blobs in the top panes and gradually ease off towards the bottom of the window, leaving white space to illustrate the effect of bright sunlight bouncing off the window sill.*

*Shading and dark shadows are achieved with close lines and cross-hatching.*

*A few squiggles of grass and a slight thickening at the base of the tree and the lamppost gives them a feeling of belonging to the ground.*

*A few suggested wispy cracks in pavement joints is quite enough to hint at what the surface is meant to be.*

## Light and shade

I cannot emphasize enough the importance of light and shade effects. A drawing which ignores shadows looks flat and rather dull, whereas one that includes them has great warmth and character. The subject of light and shade is covered in greater depth in my companion volume in this series, *Drawing Light and Shade*.

*Village pump in 6B pencil on cartridge paper. In this sketch I drew the details and features quite carefully, as an outline drawing only. But, as soon as I added the shadows the whole picture came to life and became three-dimensional.*

*In strong sunlight, notice how the cast shadows are darker than the walls and objects casting the shadows. This is due to reflected sunlight bouncing back from the immediate surroundings.*

*Cockagnes barn, Tintwistle, Derbyshire. Conté pastels, charcoal, and chalks on tinted Ingres paper. Strong shadows give shape and composition to the stone buildings. The dark areas help to sculpture the surface and give added depth to all recesses, including the doorways and windows. Notice how the shaded foreground emphasizes the warm sunshine beyond.*

# Simple ways to achieve difficult effects

Artists who wish to sketch outdoor scenes are faced with three recurring problem areas; sky, water, and trees. This is not to suggest that other problems do not exist, but I shall deal with some of them later.

On analysis of these three problems, it seems that each involves 'suggesting' large masses of quite detailed areas. So, how can this be done? Simplicity is the golden rule and you should avoid complexity at all costs. The answer lies in deciding how much can be omitted and left to the viewer's imagination. It is necessary to give subtle indications of the terrain, and providing these clues is the skill in drawing. Any drawing or painting so complete as to show every leaf on a tree, every slate on a roof, or every ripple on water does not allow the viewer's imagination to participate. Without this stimulation the picture soon becomes tedious, being too literal and overfinished.

*Technical pen sketch on white Bristol board.*

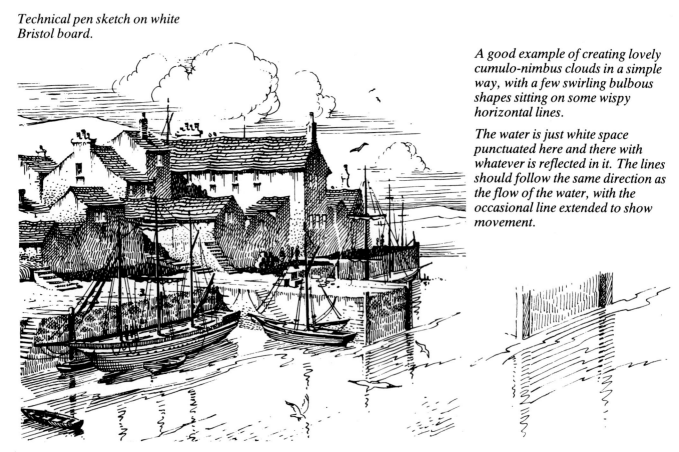

*A good example of creating lovely cumulo-nimbus clouds in a simple way, with a few swirling bulbous shapes sitting on some wispy horizontal lines.*

*The water is just white space punctuated here and there with whatever is reflected in it. The lines should follow the same direction as the flow of the water, with the occasional line extended to show movement.*

14

These two dip-pen sketches show the simple treatment of trees perfectly, with the loopy swirls of foliage on the dark shadow side of the trees only. The imagination fills in the white paper sunlit areas quite adequately.

The sky behind the ruined tower is wind-swept and it is enough to draw some long sweeping slightly curved lines at an acute diagonal which is a nice contrast to the vertical pile of the ruin. Notice how the skylines get closer together near the horizon.

Notice how the suggestion of stones near the edges and at the top and bottom helps to show what the rest of the white space represents. The cast shadows can always have more detail in them.

*Ravenglass, Cumbria. Pen and ink on Bristol board. This drawing was a good exercise in perspective. There were a lot of bits and pieces lying around, plus a profusion of detail, which I tried to suggest. Happily, it comes together to form an interesting composition. Notice how the windows facing the sun are quite dark in their reflections, whilst the windows in the shade reflect light.*

16

*Ravenglass, Cumbria. Technical pen on smooth cartridge paper.*

### Perspective

Most artists would agree that perspective provides one of the biggest challenges to their skill. Whilst many people approach the task with excitement and anticipation, others feel quite daunted by the prospect and, in some cases, purposely try to avoid anything where good perspective is needed. Bad perspective can ruin your picture no matter how much attention you pay to other details. You cannot cover it up with elaborate drawing, and it is better to have a subject that looks right, even if your finishing is somewhat lacking in expertise. Judgement based on experience will improve your perspective more effectively than learning its intricate rules.

Every year I tutor painting and drawing holiday courses in France and the major problem that confronts me is 'how can perspective be simplified?' I put myself into the position of the keen amateur who is overawed by a subject full of difficult angles, and remembering the obvious rule that everything gets smaller as it recedes from us, I devised a simple aid (see overleaf).

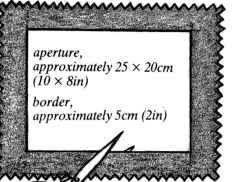

*aperture,
approximately 25 × 20cm
(10 × 8in)*

*border,
approximately 5cm (2in)*

Using thick mounting card or an old mount that you have finished with, snip out little triangular notches 6mm (¼in) deep all round.

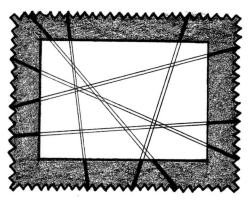

Place about six or eight thin elastic bands, capable of stretching tightly but without breaking, between any of the notches.

Sitting comfortably, with a sketch-pad or some paper taped down on to a small ply drawing board, look through the frame at arms length, as you would a viewfinder, and decide on your subject.

*ply drawing board*

*paper*

*perspective frame*

Place the frame down on to the paper and lightly draw a pencil line all round, using the inside edge of the frame. This pencil border now forms the size of your subject as seen through the frame.

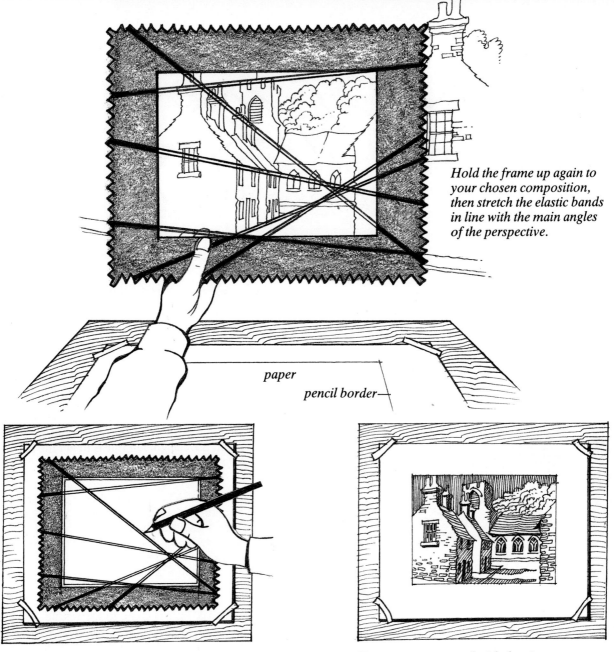

*Hold the frame up again to your chosen composition, then stretch the elastic bands in line with the main angles of the perspective.*

paper

pencil border

*Carefully replace the frame on to the paper over your pencil borderline. Next, draw the main angles of the perspective on to the paper using the elastic bands as a guide.*

*Now you can proceed with the picture.*

## Figures

There is no more depressing sight than a landscape, particularly a townscape, with not a soul in sight, just as if some awful plague had wiped everyone off the face of the earth. I do not advocate pictures crawling with people, but one or two figures in the right place add life and animation to any scene and give the subject a sense of scale.

Some artists find figures a real bugbear and avoid drawing them. I have seen numerous well-drawn pictures spoilt by poorly drawn figures, which are either artificially posed like a tailor's dummy or just look out of place. I have tried to analyse this problem and have come to the conclusion that what a lot of artists cannot quite understand is that no matter how well drawn the figure may be, if the pose is wrong then no amount of drawing skill can rescue it. I would even suggest that your talent for drawing is far less important than getting the pose right. So, the golden rule is to get the pose right first, as you can always improve your drawing ability with time and practice.

**Getting the pose right** I remember a few years ago drawing a picture of a bustling market place, thronged with customers and stall-holders. As you can imagine, trying to capture this constantly moving multitude was a real headache, even though I could draw quickly. I realized I was spending far too much time trying to sketch the fully clothed body, when I should have been concentrating on quickly capturing the pose. This is where matchstick figures came to my rescue. These are simply sketched impressions of people which, once committed to paper, can be clothed at leisure.

Earlier in the book is a drawing of a little French pavement café, so, as an example, I have drawn the two central figures from this picture in the way that I have just described.

*Matchstick figures of the customer giving his order to the waiter who is not going to hang about for long. Things to look out for in the poses are:*
1. *The tilt of the head on top of the spine.*
2. *The curvature of the spine. Is the person leaning forward or backward?*
3. *The way the arms are hanging down, pointing, pushing, pulling or gesticulating.*
4. *Are the legs straight or bent? Old people, like the waiter, have slightly bent legs.*

*Dressing the figures is quite an interesting exercise, but you must approach the task with humour. Getting the matchstick pose right is obviously very important, but still try to have fun. Quickly do as many as possible. You are bound to have a few failures at first but do not despair. I have spent many happy hours filling a page in my sketch-book with undressed matchstick figures.*

# Experimenting with textured effects

In this section I endeavour to widen the purely conventional approach to texturing by using somewhat unconventional aids.

## Cork mat

An unusual effect can be created simply by placing a cork mat under your drawing and then shading over it. Other surfaces worth trying in this way for their textures include hessian, vinyl, sandpaper, wood, and wire mesh.

Having lightly sketched my subject, I put a cork mat under the paper. Using the side of the pencil point, I shaded, with pressure, the different areas. The wall, grass, path, side of the house, and trees all achieved an interesting broken textured effect. Then, I dispensed with the cork mat and, using a sharp, soft pencil, drew in the house, windows, chimney-pots, a few pebbles, and some blades of grass. Most importantly, I picked out a few stones where the cork texture seemed to lend itself.

*A little barn and tree subject illustrates the lovely effect that can be achieved with a conté stick. I put a cork mat under the barn and tree and then used the conté pencil to emphasize the slates and stonework, plus some thin twigs. The vague background trees were drawn with conté stick over vinyl with a veined surface. Then, I used the conté pencil to suggest a few more branches and the straggly fence.*

## Ball-point pen

The clean point of a completely empty ball-point pen is an effective tool for indicating highlights in a drawing. Having lightly drawn your subject, decide on the areas which may need this kind of treatment. It may be long grasses or brambles, or the delicate veins on leaves. Perhaps some stonework needs to be accentuated here and there. To highlight these details, use pressure on the point of the pen to make a dented impression on the clean paper, then shade over the areas while you are making the picture.

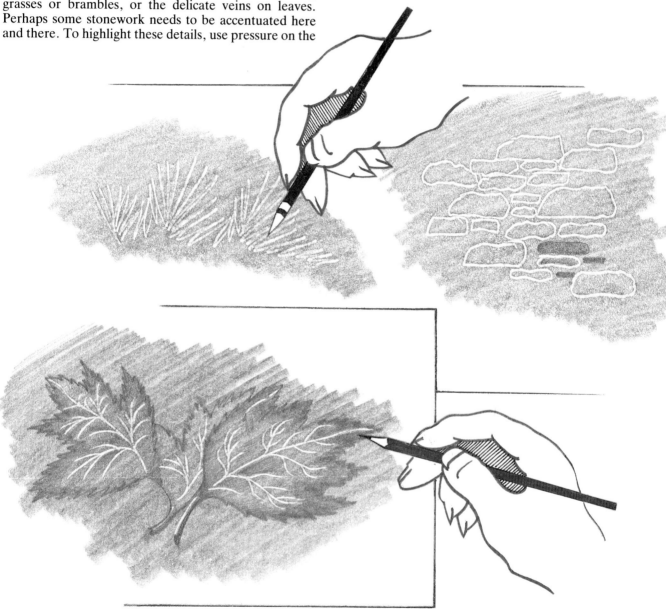

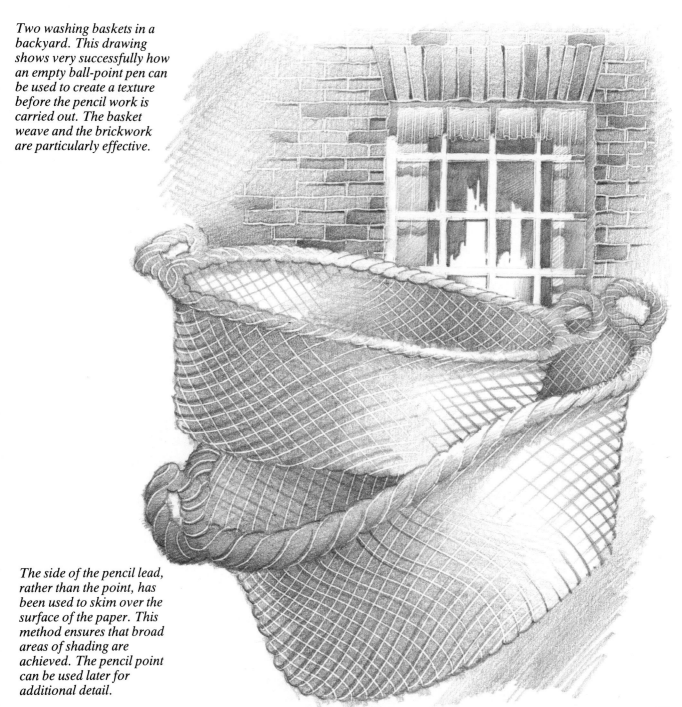

Two washing baskets in a backyard. This drawing shows very successfully how an empty ball-point pen can be used to create a texture before the pencil work is carried out. The basket weave and the brickwork are particularly effective.

The side of the pencil lead, rather than the point, has been used to skim over the surface of the paper. This method ensures that broad areas of shading are achieved. The pencil point can be used later for additional detail.

## Sponge treatments

This is one of my favourite devices and gives me some of my quickest and most effective results. For years, I have used a real sponge as opposed to the synthetic variety which is not rough enough. A real sponge has character and transfers this quality to the picture.

The secret of this method is to be quick and positive. Do not smudge or interfere with the image. The vague, rather abstract shape of trees and hedgerows lend themselves perfectly to this treatment. Having dabbed on a few watercolour or grey blobs, use a water-soluble pencil to add some branches whilst it is still wet.

I used to have a sponge which I held in my fingers to apply and a separate water-soluble pencil which was always going astray just at the vital moment, so it seemed an obvious progression to tape a good piece of rough sponge on to the end of the pencil. As well as making life easier, this also allows me to complete the treatment more quickly. After using the sponge, a deft twirl of the pencil places the lead at my fingertips.

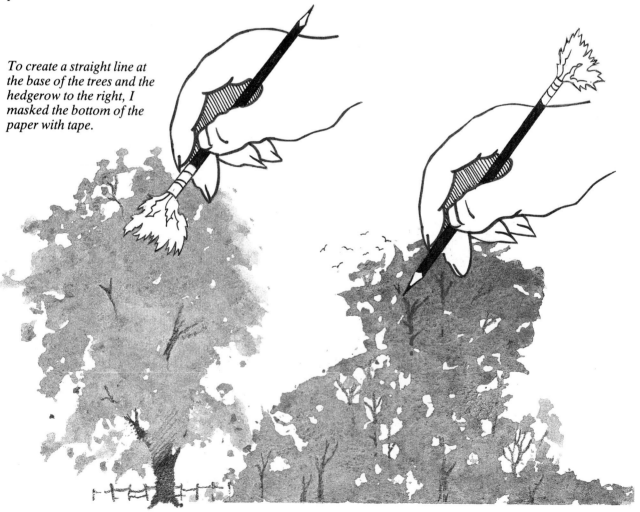

*To create a straight line at the base of the trees and the hedgerow to the right, I masked the bottom of the paper with tape.*

In this simple landscape I have been a little extravagant with my use of the sponge, in order to illustrate the extent to which the technique can be exploited. Except for the hint of farm buildings, a bit of fence, and the vague suggestion of a horse and a figure, the whole subject was completed in about twenty minutes.

Notice how I have squeezed a piece of sponge into a bulldog clip so that only a slight, ragged edge is showing. Dipped into a saucer of diluted ink or wash, this gives a wonderful, haphazard foreground of tall grasses.

27

## Feathering and spattering

The benefit of using feathering and spattering techniques is that they give a drawing done with a pencil or pen some added textures. A pen line is usually contrived and purposeful which can, on occasion, look rather formal or clinical, so anything that can be used to make an interesting, informal contribution to the subject will lend spontaneity.

One of the most pleasant and effective items to use to apply a delicate textured wash over a drawing is a long, firm feather. It is particularly suitable for tall foreground grasses and the feathery foliage of pine trees.

Spattering, as the name implies, is simply a method of scattering ink or paint over a drawing to create a rough or weathered effect, for example, on rocks or masonry.

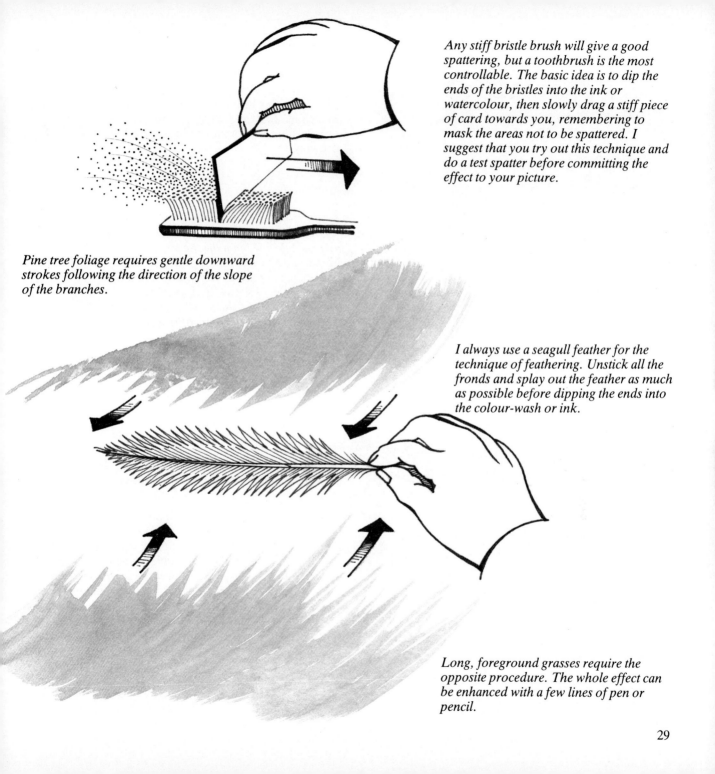

Any stiff bristle brush will give a good spattering, but a toothbrush is the most controllable. The basic idea is to dip the ends of the bristles into the ink or watercolour, then slowly drag a stiff piece of card towards you, remembering to mask the areas not to be spattered. I suggest that you try out this technique and do a test spatter before committing the effect to your picture.

Pine tree foliage requires gentle downward strokes following the direction of the slope of the branches.

I always use a seagull feather for the technique of feathering. Unstick all the fronds and splay out the feather as much as possible before dipping the ends into the colour-wash or ink.

Long, foreground grasses require the opposite procedure. The whole effect can be enhanced with a few lines of pen or pencil.

### Candle treatments

A sharpened pointed candle can be used to great effect on all paper surfaces where the finish has to look rough and broken. However, it must be used with care and discretion because once applied it cannot be removed. So, think first and then rub the candle only in those areas where you intend to brush a colour-wash over the drawing.

*After sketching out the head quickly and roughly with a waterproof ink pen, I decided that the hat and beard needed a highly textured finish. I sharpened a candle to a rounded point and then applied it with a firm, swirling, circular motion to the top of the hat and around the edges of the beard. When using the candle, I had to take care not to encroach on any area where a clean, untextured wash was required.*

*A rough-surfaced watercolour paper is ideal for this technique, and I like using Not surface Bockingford paper.*

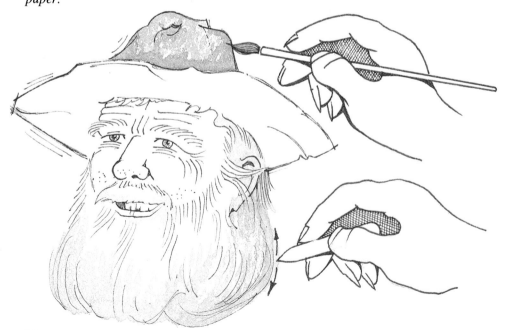

*At this stage, I mixed three different tonal values of diluted indian ink. With a sable brush I then washed over the appropriate areas, leaving the light tones where required but going over and over the patches where darker tones were needed, particularly the hat brim and the shaded forehead. As you can see, the candle wax has worked most effectively.*

*Pen, ink, and wash on Not surface Bockingford paper. The subject of this drawing is an old American tramp who agreed to pose for me whilst I was on a working trip to California.*

*I like using a candle in my drawings because it gives any washes that I put on the picture a rugged, weather-beaten look, by the simple action of the wax resisting the wash. The battered hat and scraggy beard of the tramp certainly lent themselves to this treatment.*

31

First published in Great Britain 1992
Search Press Limited,
Wellwood, North Farm Road,
Tunbridge Wells, Kent TN2 3DR

Text and drawings by Peter Caldwell

*Publishers' note*
There are references to sable hair brushes in this book. It is the Publishers' custom to recommend synthetic materials as substitutes for animal products wherever possible. There are now a large number of brushes available made of artificial fibres and they are just as satisfactory as those made of natural fibres.

ISBN 0 85532 680 8

*Distributors to the art trade:*

*UK*

Winsor & Newton,
Whitefriars Avenue, Wealdstone,
Harrow, Middlesex HA3 5RH

*USA*

ColArt Americas Inc.,
11 Constitution Avenue, P.O. Box 1396, Piscataway, NJ 08855–1396

Arthur Schwartz & Co.,
234 Meads Mountain Road, Woodstock, NY 12498

*Canada*

Anthes Universal Limited,
341 Heart Lake Road South, Brampton, Ontario L6W 3K8

*Australia*

Max A. Harrell,
P.O. Box 92, Burnley, Victoria 3121

Jasco Pty Limited,
937–941 Victoria Road, West Ryde, N.S.W. 2114

*New Zealand*

Caldwell Wholesale Limited,
Wellington and Auckland

*South Africa*

Ashley & Radmore (Pty) Limited,
P.O. Box 2794, Johannesburg 2000

Trade Winds Press (Pty) Limited,
P.O. Box 20194, Durban North 4016

Composition by Genesis Typesetting, Rochester, Kent
Printed in Spain by Elkar S. Coop.